U. S. State Quarters Explained

# U.S. State Quarters Explained

BY JESSICA A. MILLER

U. S. State Quarters Explained

Copyright © 2021 Jessica A. Miller
All rights reserved.
ISBN: 9798594353077

U. S. State Quarters Explained

# DEDICATION

Dedicated to Marcia Walters and all others that look at the world we live in with appreciation, curiosity, and wonder.

U. S. State Quarters Explained

# CONTENTS

## Contents

By Jessica A. Miller ................................................................. i
DEDICATION ...................................................................... iii
CONTENTS ........................................................................... v
ACKNOWLEDGMENTS ...................................................... ix
A Sense of Wonder ................................................................ 1
Heads on all State Quarters ................................................... 2
What is on ALL the Tails sides .............................................. 3
1 Alabama ............................................................................. 4
2 Alaska ................................................................................. 5
3 Arizona ............................................................................... 6
4 Arkansas ............................................................................. 7
5 California ........................................................................... 8
6 Colorado ............................................................................. 9
7 Connecticut ...................................................................... 10
8 Delaware .......................................................................... 11
9 Florida .............................................................................. 12
10 Georgia ........................................................................... 13
11 Hawaii ............................................................................ 14
12 Idaho .............................................................................. 15
13 Illinois ............................................................................ 16
14 Indiana ........................................................................... 17
15 Iowa ............................................................................... 18
16 Kansas ............................................................................ 19
17 Kentucky ........................................................................ 20
18 Louisiana ........................................................................ 21
19 Maine ............................................................................. 22
20 Maryland ........................................................................ 23

| | |
|---|---|
| 21 Massachusetts | 24 |
| 22 Michigan | 25 |
| 23 Minnesota | 26 |
| 24 Mississippi | 27 |
| 25 Missouri | 28 |
| 26 Montana | 29 |
| 27 Nebraska | 30 |
| 28 Nevada | 31 |
| 29 New Hampshire | 32 |
| 30 New Jersey | 33 |
| 31 New Mexico | 34 |
| 32 New York | 35 |
| 33 North Carolina | 36 |
| 34 North Dakota | 37 |
| 35 Ohio | 38 |
| 36 Oklahoma | 39 |
| 37 Oregon | 40 |
| 38 Pennsylvania | 41 |
| 39 Rhode island | 42 |
| 40 South Carolina | 43 |
| 41 South Dakota | 44 |
| 42 Tennessee | 45 |
| 43 Texas | 46 |
| 44 Utah | 47 |
| 45 Vermont | 48 |
| 46 Virginia | 49 |
| 47 Washington | 50 |
| 48 West Virginia | 51 |
| 49 Wisconsin | 52 |
| 50 Wyoming | 53 |
| ABOUT THE AUTHOR | 54 |

U. S. State Quarters Explained

U. S. State Quarters Explained

U. S. State Quarters Explained

## ACKNOWLEDGMENTS

Major resources for this book, including the picture images were USMint.gov, and Wikipedia.com, with occasional bits of information from the web sites for individual states. They have my great thanks.

## A SENSE OF WONDER

This book started as a project my mother-in-law Marcia who was collecting all the state quarters as a present for some of the younger relatives. She had been lovingly collecting quarters for years, while working at the gift store at Hearst Castle. As we were sorting through, we started asking questions on what the images on the back of each quarter meant. We looked them up and found the most amazing stories!

That is how the idea for this book was born. I found the pictures of the coins on the Wikipedia and the US Mint. I loved being able to see the detail in the much larger than actual size art and wanted to share them. Each design is a little piece of history, nature, or culture so special the residents of that state wanted to honor it.

The 50 State Quarter Program, launched in 1999, was a 10-year initiative by the United States Mint. Five quarters came out each year. Quarters were issued in the order the states joined the Union or ratified their constitution. For ease of reference, in this book they are listed alphabetically.

Many of the designs were suggested or voted on by school children. Some were chosen by the residents of the state, others by state governments.

Writing this book was my way of connecting to the diversity of our country, appreciation for where we been and hope for where we are going.

It is my hope this book will surprise and delight you. I certainly learned a lot writing it! I hope all of you will experience the same sense of wonder we have had as you read this book.

Jessica Miller
Jan 22, 2021
Cambria, CA

## HEADS ON ALL STATE QUARTERS

Did you know George Washington has been on the heads (obverse) side of all US Quarters since George Washington's 2000th birthday in 1932?

"United States of America" is of course the issuing country of origin. "Quarter Dollar" reflects its value of 25 cents, one quarter of a dollar.

"In God We Trust" has been the official motto of the United States since 1956. (see next page) "Liberty" has appeared on all US coins since 1793.

The single letter that appears on any US coin is the mint where it was made. P-Philadelphia Mint, D-Denver Mint or S-San Francisco Mint.

## WHAT IS ON ALL THE TAILS SIDES

To simplify the state quarter descriptions in this book, lets first focus on what features appear on the tails (reverse) side of ALL of the state quarters, using California as an example. The name of the state appears at the top, followed by the year it entered the union or ratified their constitution.

On the bottom of the coin is the year the state quarter was issued. Below it is the phrase "E Pluribus Unum." This is Latin for "Out of Many, One" and was the official the motto of the United States until 1956, when it was replaced by "In God We Trust". Efforts have been made to return to the original Latin motto, including in 2011 and 2006, but have failed.

The dark area of the coin picture is an artistic rendering of the reflection of the metal and makes the designs easier to see.

Some coins also have the initials of the coin designer, who I have specified if there is room in the text.

# 1 ALABAMA

Alabama's quarter is titled "Spirit of Courage". The seated figure is Helen Keller (1880-1968), the famous Alabama blind and deaf girl that learned sign language as a child. Helen's name appears in both English and Braille on the coin. On the left of the coin is a branch of the state tree, the long leaf pine. On the right is the state flower, the camellia.

Helen Keller's passionate determination to defy stereotypes for the disabled led her to become the first deaf and blind woman to graduate from college in the United States. She was an advocate for women's suffrage (right to vote,) an early member of the American Civil Liberties Union and worked for 40 years for the American Foundation for the Blind. She was an outspoken pacifist, socialist and worker's rights activist who influenced legislation, health care, and many other causes. She visited 35 countries and 5 continents and was prolific author and speaker.

## 2 ALASKA

Alaska's quarter is titled "The Great Land." The name Alaska is based on the Aleut word meaning Great Land or Mainland. Alaska's focus on the outdoors is conveyed by the grizzly bear catching a salmon in a wild river near a waterfall. This iconic image expresses the states natural beauty, resourcefulness, and wild spirit. There are about 50,000 grizzly bears in the state, and the 2019 salmon season was worth 657.6 million to fishermen.

The North Star, Polaris appears above the inscription and to the right of the name of the state. Because of its alignment with the earth's axis, Polaris does not rise or set, but remains in the same spot in the sky year-round.

CLV are the initials of the coin designer Charles Vickers, who designed 35+ coins and medals for the US mint, including several other state quarters.

## 3 ARIZONA

Arizona's nickname is the "Grand Canyon State." The Grand Canyon is a mile deep, 227 miles long and 18 miles wide. The park was protected as a Forest Reserve in 1893, and in 1919 became a national park. Popular even in 1919, it received 44,173 visitors, many who came on its special train built in 1901. The number of annual visitors now is typically around 5 million.

The quarter depicts the rays of the sun shining on the Grand Canyon. The canyon in in the northern part of the state, 80 miles from Flagstaff. The southern part of the state is honored below the banner. The famous saguaro cactus grows in the Phoenix area and further south. Also shown as part of the desert landscape are the well-known prickly pear cactus and yucca plants, both of which are edible.

## 4 ARKANSAS

The Arkansas coin focuses on the state's natural resources. It features rice stalks, a diamond, and a mallard flying above a lake bordered by pines.

Rice is the state grain. First planted in South Carolina in the 1690s, it was cultivated in Arkansas in small amounts by 1840 but did not become a major crop until the early 1900s. Arkansas is now the biggest rice producer in the United States, with 1.1 million acres in cultivation.

Arkansas has the only producing diamond mine in the United States. It is an old volcanic cone, now broken up into a field in the south western part of the state at the Crater of Diamonds state park. It is the only diamond mine in the world where the public can pay an entrance fee and mine diamonds. The state is also popular for hunting natural quartz crystals.

# 5 CALIFORNIA

The California quarter depicts John Muir, the noted naturalist and conservationist, admiring Half Dome rock in his beloved Yosemite Valley. John Muir was the leader of the Western Preservationist Movement which led to Yosemite becoming a national park in 1890. His books, articles, quotes, and paintings inspired the world to appreciate wilderness. "In every walk with nature one receives far more than he seeks."

A California condor soars overhead on the coin. The adult California condor has the largest wingspan of any North American bird, at nearly 10 feet. This amazing bird went extinct in the wild in 1987 due to habitats loss and the chemical DDT. (The last 27 were caught.) Environmental legislation conservation, and captive breeding programs, are restoring the birds to the wild, where there are now more than 300 breeding pairs.

## 6 COLORADO

The Colorado coin depicts the rugged Rocky Mountain range, with its evergreen trees. The banner says, 'Colorful Colorado." The name Colorado comes from the Spanish word for 'colored red' referring to the reddish mud color of the Colorado river. Colorful can also apply to the state's majestic snowcapped mountains, rivers, plains, and even sand dunes.

The Rocky Mountain range dominates most of the state. Denver is on a high plain a mile (5280 ft) above sea level. Because of these mountains, Colorado's climate ranges from the semi-arid grass plains to forests to alpine tundra. Warm Pacific air pushed upward by mountains means that much of Colorado gets 60-100 inches of snow per year. The Great Divide is the section of the mountains that divides the country into eastern and western watersheds. At the highest point, the divide is 14, 278 feet high.

## 7 CONNECTICUT

Connecticut's quarter features a famous oak tree that grew in the Hartford area near the Connecticut river, estimated to have been 1000 years old. Long before colonial settlement, the oak was a place of meeting for Native American councils, Sadly, the charter oak fell during a rain and wind storm in 1856. Artifacts made from the wood appear in Connecticut museums

The charter that "Charter Oak" refers to is the original charter to settle the colony issued in 1662 by King Charles of England. When the king died, his brother James demanded the charter's return so he could rewrite its laws. Legend says in 1687, there was a fierce argument about the charter between the royal governor and the colony leaders. It happened during a fierce thunderstorm, the candles blew out and the colony charter disappeared. It was found 2 years later in the trunk of this majestic white oak.

## 8 DELAWARE

The design of the coin celebrates Caesar Rodney's historic ride that led to the founding of the nation. He got word his vote would be desperately needed. Caesar Rodney rode eighty miles at night through summer heat and thunderstorms to arrive in time to cast his vote in favor of Delaware signing the Declaration of Independence. His vote was the tiebreaker that resulted in the creation of the United states on July 4 1776.

Caesar Rodney had many roles in his long life of public service. He served as a Sheriff, a Justice of the Peace, an Assemblymen, an associate Justice on the state Supreme Court, Speaker of the State Legislature, Delegate to the Continental Congress, and President of the State.

## 9 FLORIDA

Florida's coin is called Gateway to Discovery. It symbolizes the state's connection to the explorations of the past and the future. It shows the galleon ship and the space shuttle, both touching Florida's shore and palms.

The galleon ship is from Ponce de Leon's discovery of what is now Florida in 1513. This Spanish explorer came with Christopher Columbus on his second voyage in 1493. Leon was later the first governor of Puerto Rico.

The space shuttle flew 135 missions from the Kennedy Space Center at Cape Canaveral near Orlando between 1981 and 2011. The shuttle and its astronauts launched numerous satellites, conducted science experiments, and participated in the construction and servicing of the International Space station.

## 10 GEORGIA

Georgia's quarter features the state's motto "Wisdom, Justice, Moderation" the peach, and a silhouette outline of the state. The leaves are of the state tree, the Quercus Virginiana or Southern Live Oak. Live Oaks are oaks that do not lose their leaves in the wintertime. There are many live oak species.

The state motto adopted in 1799 refers to the guiding principles of the three branches of government. Wisdom to guide the legislature, Justice the judiciary branch and Moderation for the executive branch.

Peaches are the Georgia state fruit. Peaches originated in China in ancient times. They were brought to North America, including Georgia, by Spanish Monks in the mid-1500s. Georgia grown peaches are renowned for their terrific flavor and are featured at many Georgia festivals and events.

## 11 HAWAII

Hawaii's coin honors the famous Hawaiian King, Kamehameha I (1782-1819). Hawaii was originally settled by the Polynesians over 1000 years ago and was a series of separate city island states.

Kamehameha unified the Hawaiian Islands in the early 1800s through a series of wars. A harsh and deadly warrior, he had a life changing experience when injured in a raid and left for dead. Thereafter his new law became "Let every elderly person, woman and child lie by the roadside in safety." He also supported Hawaiians embracing their native traditions.

The coin depicts him stretching his hand out towards the 8 main Hawaiian islands. The state motto UA MAU KE EA O KA ' AINA I KA PONO," means "The life of the land is perpetuated in righteousness."

U. S. State Quarters Explained

## 12 IDAHO

Idaho' quarter features the Peregrine falcon, one of the fastest birds in the world, able to dive at speeds of over 200 miles to an hour. The peregrine is the 'state raptor'. Idaho is only state with a state Raptor, as well as a state bird. Peregrines were essentially extinct in Idaho by 1974 due to DDT chemical accumulation. Eliminating the chemical, and a captive breeding program has allowed the bird to be reintroduced, and there are now several dozen wild breeding pairs in the state.

Next to the falcon on the coin is a silhouette of the shape of the state, with a star over the state capital of Boise. The state motto "Esto Perpetua" translates from Latin as "May it be Forever." The odd shape of the state was set by congress when creating the neighboring states of Wyoming, Washington and Montana in the 1860s.

## 13 ILLINOIS

The Illinois coin features a young Abraham Lincoln standing inside the state's outline. Illinois is where Abraham Lincoln started his political career. Lincoln had taught himself law, served in the state general assembly, and became a US congressman before becoming the 16th US president in 1861. Lincoln became president shortly before the civil war, and his Emancipation Proclamation paved the way for the abolition of slavery. Land of Lincoln has been the official state motto since 1955.

The scene to the left of the state outline depicts a farm, showing Illinois agricultural roots, and to the right is the Chicago skyline. Illinois became a state in 1818 and was the 21st state admitted to the Union, and thus 21 stars on the coin and the coin motto '21st state." 21st Century also implies it is a modern state, i.e. a state of the 21st century.

## 14 INDIANA

Indiana was the 19th state admitted to the union in 1816, and thus there are 19 stars on the coin. The design features a textured shape of the state and a race car. The initials DW stand for artist Donna Weaver who designed over 40 coins and medals for the US Mint, including other state quarters.

The Indianapolis Motor Speedway was built in 1909 to test cars. Car races have been held every year since 1911 except during the two World Wars. The 2020 race was held without fans due to the pandemic.

The state motto "Crossroads of America" came from Indiana's role of being the hub of major roads that connected the country east to west (Highway 40, originally the National Trail) and north to south (Highway 41) These highways were made part of the original US highway system in 1926.

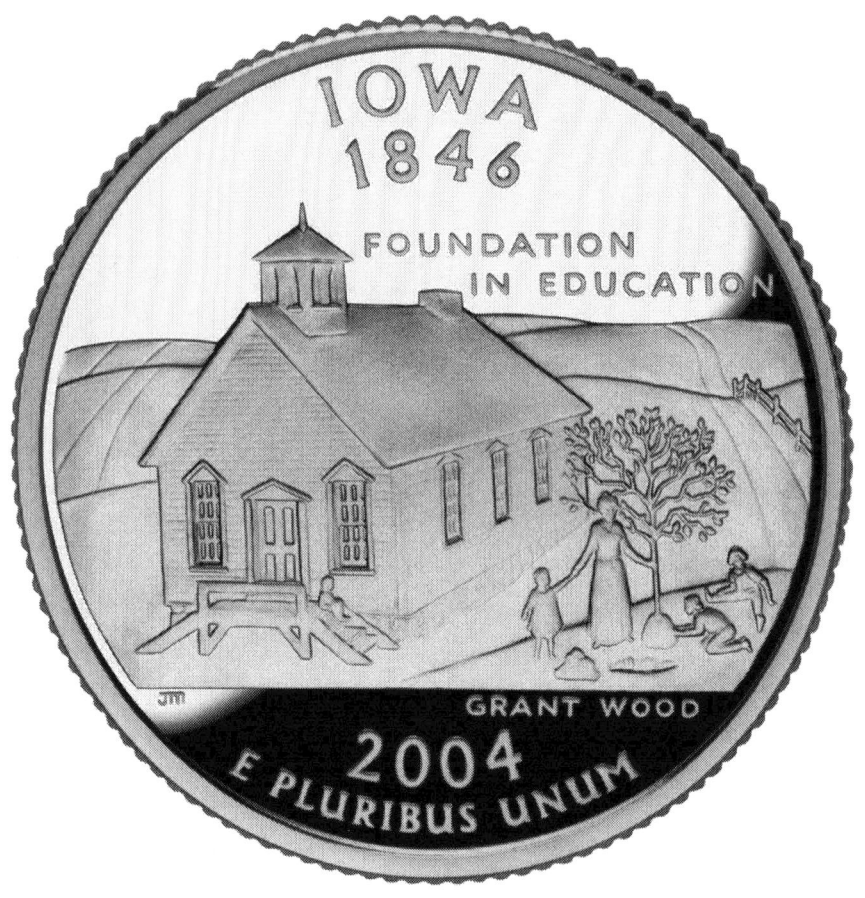

## 15 IOWA

The design of the Iowa coin is based on the painting "Arbor Day" by Iowa resident Grant Wood. The coin depicts a teacher and her students planting a tree near the country schoolhouse.

Grant Wood was most famous for the painting American Gothic (1930) and other works depicting the American rural Midwest. He was a proponent of small-town values and vistas.

The state motto, "Foundation in Education" refers to the state's strong commitment to education. Even back in 1846, when it joined the union, Iowa had multiple rural county schools. It had a high school in the 1850s even though high schools did not become common in the United States until after 1900. The state also had many early public and private colleges.

## 16 KANSAS

The sunflower and the buffalo on the Kansas quarter are two of the states most beloved symbols.

The wild sunflower, Helianthus annuus, is native to the state. The seeds have been used as a native food plant, and domesticated varieties are used for cooking oil, biodiesel fuel, and snacking.

The American bison is more commonly called the buffalo. Buffalo once roamed great plains states like Kansas by the millions. They were hunted heavily by settlers and hunters. They lost habitat to farms and ranches. Buffalo nearly became extinct, with only about 500 left in the early 1900s. Thanks to breeding and conservation programs, many started in Kansas, there are now about 200,000 animals, mostly on specialty farms and parks.

## 17 KENTUCKY

The thoroughbred horse on Kentucky's coin reflects the state's long horse racing tradition. The Kentucky Derby is one of the world's most famous horse races, having run annually for 144 years.

The grassy field on the coin is blue grass. Blue grass is not blue, but emerald green, But if it grows to full height has blue flower heads. Blue grass is not native to the America but was imported from northern Europe for animal fodder and grazing.

The mansion in the background is in Bardstown, where the abolitionist inspired song "My Old Kentucky Home" was written in 1853 by Stephen Foster. Foster wrote more than 200 songs including many still popular today including "Oh Susanna," "Swanee River," and "Beautiful Dreamer."

## 18 LOUISIANA

The Louisiana coin features the shape of the Louisiana Purchase, which almost doubled the size of the United States in 1803. The part of the purchase below the border line is the current shape of the state.

The trumpet blowing notes symbolizes New Orleans and the beginning of jazz in the late 1800s. Jazz was a blending of European classical music with African & Caribbean and Gospel elements. New Orleans jazz is big, energetic, "good time" music often played at public events including dances, ball games, festivals, and funerals.

The Pelican is the state bird. Pelicans are amazing birds to watch. Clumsy on land, they are strong swimmers and flyers. They hunt by using their beaks to scoop up fish, crustaceans, and occasionally other small animals.

## 19 MAINE

The Main coin focuses on the state's maritime connections. The lighthouse is the Pemaquid Point Light house which was built in 1826 and is still operational today. Maine currently has 65 lighthouses, signaling to sailors the location of the mouth of its harbors. Many of the lighthouses are tourist destinations open to the public.

The ship is modeled on the Victory Chimes passenger sailing ship, originally built in 1900 and still sailing today. From the ship's website: "the Victory Chimes is a three-masted, gaff-rigged Chesapeake Ram schooner, home-ported in Rockland, Maine."

Note the date of joining the union is 1820. Maine both is and is NOT one of the original 13 colonies because it was originally part of Massachusetts.

U. S. State Quarters Explained

## 20 MARYLAND

The Maryland Coin features the dome of its statehouse, the oldest state capital building still in use by any state legislature. Built in the late 1700s, various delays meant it took over 20 years to complete, but it has been in continuous operation ever since. The dome was built without any nails, just wood pegs and iron straps hold the intricate structure together.

"The Old Line State" is the state nickname given during the American Revolution, and used by George Washington. The Maryland Line were the Maryland regular regimental troops and were considered the saviors of the Continental army. 'Old' here means trusted, in the sense of "Old Reliable."

The branches to each side of the coin are oak, the state tree.

U. S. State Quarters Explained

## 21 MASSACHUSETTS

The Massachusetts coin depicts the state, including the offshore islands of Martha's Vineyard and Nantucket. A star shows the location of Boston, the state capital.

The figure is the famous statue of a Minuteman at Minuteman National Park in Concord, Mass, where the Revolutionary War began in April 1775 The Minutemen were a militia of farmers and other colonists that fought the British during the Revolutionary War. Minutemen were so named because while they were civilians that worked normal jobs in the area, as a militia they always at the ready, and able to assemble and fight in minutes.

The state's nickname, "The Bay State" refers to the large bay inside the curve of Cape Cod. The original British Royal Charter of 1629 establishing the colony referred to it as the "Massachusetts Bay Colony."

## 22 MICHIGAN

Michigan's quarter shows a relief map of the state, an outline of the Great Lakes, and the motto "The Great Lakes State." The Great Lakes combined make up the largest body of fresh water in the world and play a major role in the Michigan and US economy. Lake Michigan is over 100 miles wide and 300 miles long. Lake Superior alone is the world's largest freshwater lake by surface area, being bigger than the combined areas of Connecticut, New Hampshire, Rhode Island, Massachusetts, and Vermont.

Michigan consists of the 'Mitten' and the unattached Upper Peninsula. The Peninsula was added as part of a US Congressional compromise over Michigan's southern boundary with Ohio, when Michigan became a state. Ohio got the 'Toledo strip" and Michigan got the upper Peninsula.

## 23 MINNESOTA

Inside the outline of the state on the coin is the motto "Land of 10,000 Lakes" This is an understatement. If one includes all the basins of water bigger than 2.5 acres (about 2 football fields) in cities and 10 acres or more in rural areas Minnesota has close to 12,000 lakes. The 10,000 lakes idea was popularized in the 1920s by the state tourist agency who had not counted.

The pine trees, lake, and people fishing focus on Minnesota's natural resources. The state bird floating in the foreground is the loon.

Virtually all of Minnesota's cultivatable prairies and forests were cleared for farms in the late 19th and early 20th century. But as patterns of agriculture changed, most of the northern less fertile part of the state have reverted to forests of pine, birch, aspen, balsam and spruce, now a forested paradise.

# U. S. State Quarters Explained

## 24 MISSISSIPPI

The Mississippi's state coin features the state flower, the Magnolia. It is also the state flower of neighboring Louisiana, although it does not appear on its coin. The Magnolia symbolizes dignity, nobility, purity, and gentleness.

Magnolias are an ancient genus of tree that originated before bees evolved and were around during the time of the dinosaurs. Their flowers petals are exceptionally tough to handle being pollinated by beetles. Varieties of magnolia are native to North America, Central America, South America, and the West Indies.

The Magnolia Grandiflora or Southern magnolia is native to the South Eastern US. It has creamy, fragrant, white flowers up to a foot in diameter from May to Late June. Trees grow 60-80 feet high, and 35-40 feet wide.

## 25 MISSOURI

The Missouri state coin features the 'Corps of Discovery." The corps was a US Army special unit led by Lewis and Clark from 1804-1806 consisting of soldiers, mountain men and American Indians.

Captain Meriwether Lewis and Second Lieutenant William Clark were commissioned by President Thomas Jefferson to explore the enormous Louisiana purchase which nearly doubled the size of the country in 1803. The Corp was dedicated to researching its plants, animal life and geography.

The coin depicts Lewis and Clarks return to St Louis down the Missouri river. The Gateway Arch is in the background, part of the Gateway Arch National Park, built 1963-1965, to honor the westward expansion for which the Lewis and Clark mission helped lay the foundation.

U. S. State Quarters Explained

## 26 MONTANA

Montana's coin features the mountains and plains of the Montana landscape with the Missouri river running through it, a buffalo skull, and the state's nickname "Big Sky Country."

The Buffalo (American Bison) skull symbolizes the connections to the American Indian tribes of the area who used buffalo for food, clothing, and shelter. The buffalo skull symbol appears on many Montana schools, businesses and license plates and road signs.

Big Sky Country refers to Montana's many wide-open spaces with unobstructed often dramatic skies that seem to dominate the landscape, and low population density. There are about 1 million people in the state, or an average of 7 people/square mile (California is 246, Rhode Island is 1017.)

## 27 NEBRASKA

The Nebraska coins features an ox-drawn wagon carrying pioneers past Chimney Rock, during America's westward expansion. Nebraska's heritage as a major travel pathway is still traceable, with Oregon and Mormon trails, The Pony Express, Lewis and Clark Trail and more still in existence.

Chimney Rock was the most famous landmark along the Oregon Trail. It stands nearly 300 feet high in a valley of the North Platte River. Created by natural erosion, this formation can be seen from over 30 miles away.

Between the 1830s and the 1870s, nearly 400,000 people traveled the Oregon Trail, making it the largest voluntary migration in human history. They included miners, ranchers, farmers, business owners and families. Oxen and mules pulled many of the wagons on a typically 5-month journey.

## 28 NEVADA

Nevada's quarter features 3 wild mustangs. Nevada is home to over half of the country's wild horses. Mustangs are the descendants of Spanish or Iberian horses brought to the western United States by 16th century Spanish Explorers. These horses later mixed with other feral horses in the old west.

The branches to either side of the coin are sage brush, which is the state flower. Some of Nevada's many mountains appear in the background with the rays of the setting sun. The name Nevada comes from the Spanish word that means 'snowcapped' referring to its tall snowcapped mountains.

"The Silver State" refers to the silver found near Virginia city during the mid-1800s "Silver Rush." Silver was found in many parts of the state, including Comstock, Austin, Reese, and Pioche. Gold was also found.

## 29 NEW HAMPSHIRE

The New Hampshire quarter shows its most famous natural rock formation. The formation was 25 feet wide and 40 feet in Franconia Notch, in the northern part of the state. Natural forces of freeze and thaw finally took their toll on the formation, which collapsed in 2003.

The Old Man of the Mountain was made famous by New Hampshire native statesman Daniel Webster who wrote: "Men hang out their signs indicative of their respective trades; shoemakers hang out a gigantic shoe; jewelers a monster watch, and the dentist hangs out a gold tooth; but up in the Mountains of New Hampshire, God Almighty has hung out a sign to show that there He makes men."

The state motto "Live Free or Die" was a motto taken from a toast made by New Hampshire Revolutionary war general John Stark.

U. S. State Quarters Explained

## 30 NEW JERSEY

The New Jersey coin depicts George Washington leading his troops across the half-frozen Delaware river on Christmas night 1776. This positioned troops and their artillery to win several key battles against the British in Trenton and Princeton in the following 10 days. These key battles are the origin of the state's 'crossroads of the revolution' motto.

The coin is based on the famous painting "Washington Crossing the Delaware". This is one of the most famous paintings about one of the most iconic events in the American revolution, yet it was painted in Germany by a German artists, Emanuel Leutze to inspire German political reform. The painting is 21 feet wide and 12 feet high. It is on display at the Metropolitan Museum of Art in New York City. The figures in the boat depict the variety of men that joined the revolution, from many nations and social classes.

U. S. State Quarters Explained

## 31 NEW MEXICO

The New Mexico quarter feature a topographical map of the state, with the Zia Pueblo Indian sun symbol centered on the capital, Santa Fe. The state motto, "Land of Enchantment" refers to the state's distinctive natural beauty, culture, architecture, and cuisine. It is a unique mix of European, Native American, and Mexican cultures. New Mexico has snowcapped mountains and hot springs, deserts, and national monuments.

The Zia Sun Symbol appears everywhere in New Mexico: on the flag, license plates, and signs. While there is some debate on whether it is a traditional Zia symbol, the design visually evokes the Zia connection to the sun, and the spiritual significance of the number four. Four can represent the four directions, the four seasons, and the four sacred obligations: strong body, clear mind, pure spirit, and devotion to welfare of people.

## 32 NEW YORK

New York's quarter features the Statue of Liberty, a topographic map of the state inset with a line representing the Erie Canal. The Erie Canal propelled the state's growth in the early 1800s for commercial shipping. The eleven stars indicate New York was the 11th state to join the union.

The Statue of Liberty and the Motto "Gateway to Freedom", celebrate the millions of immigrants from all over that world that arrived in the United States via neighboring Ellis Island. The statue was a gift from France, dedicated in 1886 to commemorate the alliance of France and the United States during the American Revolution.

The statue was originally the reddish brown of a penny. Bronze weathers greenish blue over time. She was shipped from France in 350 pieces that took 6 months to put together. The statue unveiled in October 1886.

## 33 NORTH CAROLINA

North Carolina's quarter highlights the first ever airplane flight by Orville and Wilbur Wright in 1903, near Kitty Hawk, North Carolina. The coin symbolizes North Carolina ingenuity and the origin of aviation industry.

Orville flew the plane "Flyer", and his brother Wilber was the mechanic that designed it. The first flight traveled about 120 feet in 12 seconds. It was flown in North Carolina but was actually built in Ohio (see quarter.)

The image on the coin is based on John T Daniels famous photograph of the plane in midflight. The brothers had shown Daniels, who had never taken a picture before, how to use the camera minutes before the flight.

### 34 NORTH DAKOTA

North Dakota's quarter feature a pair of Buffalo (American Bison) against the backdrop of sunset over the state's Badlands region.

The Badlands are a dramatic terrain made of colorful layers of soft rock and clay rich soil that has been extensively carved and eroded by millions of years of wind and water. The name was given by the Lakota Indians that called the area the badlands because the rocky terrain, lack of water, vegetation and extreme temperatures made travel difficult.

President Theodore Roosevelt loved the badlands since his first 2 week hunting trip there in 1883. He founded the United States Forest Service in 1906, to preserve unspoiled natural places like it. Herds of wild Buffalo roam what is now called the "Theodore Roosevelt National Park."

## 35 OHIO

In addition to the state outline, and its date of joining the union in 1803, the Ohio quarter focuses on its place as the "Birthplace of Aviation Pioneers."

The first airplane flight was made in North Carolina (see quarter) but much of the plane was made in the Orville brothers bicycle workshop in Ohio, and later designs were flown in the state. The plane depicted is an improved successor to the original plane, named the 1905 Wright Brothers III.

The Astronaut symbolizes Ohio's contribution to space aviation. Ohio native John Glenn was the first American to orbit the earth and to walk on the moon. Nineteen other Ohio residents have been to space. Four Ohio State quarters were carried to space on the Space Shuttle Columbia in 2002.

## 36 OKLAHOMA

The Oklahoma state quarter focuses on two species emblematic of its prairies: the scissortail flycatcher bird, and the Indian Blanket flower.

The Scissortail Flycatcher is the Oklahoma state bird. It is shown in flight, showing its distinctive forked tail which can reach 9" in length, nearly the length of the bird itself. The bird is a sign of spring, migrating from Central and South America. The birds are acrobatic foragers of insects and are well known for their elaborate courtship dance.

Around the bird on the coin is the Oklahoma state wildflower, The Indian Blanket, also called a Firewheel (Gaillardia pulchella). This member of the daisy family has a yellow center rimmed in red, surrounded by red petals with bright yellow tips, and thrives in Oklahoma's hot and arid conditions.

## 37 OREGON

Oregon's state quarter features Crater Lake. The lake was formed from the crater of an extinct volcano. This volcano exploded and caved in more than 8000 years ago, creating a bowl-shaped crater, filled in by rain. The lake is surrounded by fir trees, and Wizard Island is the cinder cone appearing in the center. It is part of Crater Lake National Park north of Klamath Falls.

Crater Lake is the deepest lake in the United States, and one of the 10 deepest lakes in the world. It is 1949 feet deep. [Lake Superior is 1332 feet deep.] Crater Lake is also known for the crystal clarity of its water. Water clarity was traditionally measured by submerging a white dinner plate until it disappears. At Crater Lake this is nearly 100 feet deep. The water's clarity and bright blue color is from the purity of the water, which is from rain and melted snow only, there are no streams or creeks into or out of the lake.

## 38 PENNSYLVANIA

Pennsylvania's quarter features the statue "Commonwealth" that has been on top of state capital since 1905. Her right hand is extended in benediction. The left hand holds a staff with topped by an eagle with outstretched ribbons symbolizing justice. Beside the statue is the state's motto "Virtue, Liberty and Independence."

The other image in the state outline is a keystone. The state's nickname is the "Keystone state" which originated when Thomas Jefferson's party toasted Pennsylvania as the "keystone in the federal union." In 1802. The Keystone is the wedge-shaped top block in an archway that locks all the other stones into place, without which the arch will collapse.

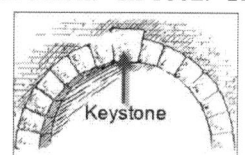

## 39 RHODE ISLAND

The Rhode Island state quarter honors its place as "The Ocean State," The image shows a sailboat gliding through Narragansett Bay, past the Pell bridge which links Newport and Jamestown.

Ocean bays and inlets make up about 14% of the states total area. Even though it is the smallest size state in the nation in size, (48 miles by 37 miles.) Rhode Island has 400 miles of coastline and has been home to the prestigious America's Cup sailboat race for more than 50 years.

Rhode Island is not that small in population, it is the 2nd densest state in the union (after New Jersey) and is 45th in population, having more people than Delaware, North and South Dakota, Alaska, Vermont, or Wyoming.

U. S. State Quarters Explained

## 40 SOUTH CAROLINA

The South Carolina quarter has a map outline of the state, with a star over Columbia, its capital. The quarter also features the state tree, the palmetto palm, and the state bird, the Carolina Wren.

Palmetto logs and fronds were used by native people in precolonial times and were used to absorb impact of Cannon balls in 1776 at Fort Moultrie.

The Carolina Wren was adopted as the state bird in 1948 and is found in a wide variety of habitats. This small bird builds its homes in holes of trees, fence posts, and the eaves of houses and barns. They live year-round in Carolina, but also most of the east coast of the country, and west to Texas. They are recognizable by the white stripe over the eye and tail up posture.

U. S. State Quarters Explained

### 41 SOUTH DAKOTA

South Dakota's quarter features Mount Rushmore, with its sculpture of four American presidents. It took 14 years to sculpt and was completed in 1941. Each face is about 60 feet high. It was originally conceived of in 1923 to promote tourism to the state. The presidents were chosen because of their impact on US history. George Washington (founder), Thomas Jefferson (Louisiana Purchase), Theodore Roosevelt (parks/pro-worker), and Abraham Lincoln (keeping country together/ending slavery.)

The Chinese ring-necked pheasant is the state bird. This colorful bird was imported to the state in 1898 for sportsman and was eaten as a delicacy. No breed of pheasants is native to North America.

The wheat stalks honor the state grain, which is grown on 1.3 million acres.

U. S. State Quarters Explained

## 42 TENNESSEE

Tennessee's quarter is titled "Musical Heritage." The state has an international reputation as an important musical center. The three stars and musical instruments represent the three areas of the state, and three different popular music traditions.

The guitar is for the country music of Nashville, central Tennessee. Most well-known for "The Grand Ole Opry" So much music happens here (including other types), the city's nickname is "Music City, USA."

The trumpet stands for the Blues music of western Tennessee and the city of Memphis. Memphis is considered the "Birthplace of Rock and Roll."

The fiddle stands for the Blue Grass music of east Tennessee, and the old-time music, the Appalachian folk music tradition.

## 43 TEXAS

The Texas features a map of the state, its motto of "The Lone Star State" and a giant "lone star." The lariat rope on the sides reflects the state's frontier spirit of cowboys and cattle.

The name Lone Star state came from the flag for the Republic of Texas., which had a red stripe, a white stripe, and a blue section with a single white star. Texas won its freedom from Mexico in 1836, under General Sam Houston. Houston had been defeated badly in a far more famous battle earlier that year at the Alamo Mission in San Antonio, but at the San Jacinto were victorious, and achieved Texas independence.

The Republic of Texas was a separate country from 1836-1845 when it joined the US, in a complex story involving international pressures, secret negotiations, presidential elections and the future of slavery.

U. S. State Quarters Explained

## 44 UTAH

The Utah state coin is called "Crossroads of the West." It features the moment in 1896, the same year as statehood, when the first transcontinental Railroad track was completed. It shows East and West bound trains facing each other and the golden spike that joined the tracks.

Invented in the late 1700s, Railroads were major carriers of people and goods in the Eastern States by the mid-1800s. It was a major driver of the Industrial Revolution, but the west was too big for a private funded project.

The Union Pacific and Central Pacific railways, guaranteed loans and land through the Pacific Railroad act, from Omaha Nebraska to Sacramento, California, laid over 1000 miles of track through the west, racing to finish in Promontory Point, Utah, commemorating it with a golden railway spike.

## 45 VERMONT

Vermont's quarter shows Sugar Maple's being tapped for maple Syrup. Camel Hump Mountain is in the background. The state Motto "Freedom and Unity" appears on the right.

Maple syrup is made from the sap of the sugar maple, a type of maple that only grows in the north east portion of the continent. The trees store sap in the roots in the winter, and in the early spring, is drawn up into the tree to allow the leaves to bud and grow.

Taps are put into the trees to drain off some of the sap into buckets which is taken away to be boiled to concentrate the sugars. It takes about 40 gallons of sap to make one gallon of finished syrup. Early in the season, the sap produces a light colored 'Grade A' delicately flavored syrup, later in season it is darker, grittier with more robust flavor and minerals 'Grade B."

## 46 VIRGINIA

Jamestown, Virginia celebrated its 400th anniversary as a colony in 2007.

The coin depicts the ships that brought the first English colonists to American shore in 1607. These ships were the Susan Constant, the Godspeed, and the Discovery. The voyage took four and a half months, from December to May and carried 104 men, boys, and cargo. Women eventually came to the colony, but even in 1620, the colony was 6 to 1 male.

The Jamestown colony was established 13 years before the colony in Plymouth Massachusetts. Jamestown was named in honor of King James I, who had chartered their voyage.

## 47 WASHINGTON

Washington State's quarter has a king salmon leaping out of the water with Mount Rainier in the background.

The salmon is a symbol of Pacific Northwest culture, prized for food and recreation, now and by native peoples. Salmon live most of their lives in salt water but spawn in fresh water.

The state nickname as the "Evergreen State" was coined by a former newspaper man turned real estate agent, because of the state's lush evergreen forests. CT Conover and his business partner published a pamphlet "Washington: The Evergreen State, and Seattle, its Metropolis" in 1889, a few months after statehood. They spent $30,000 dollars (over $800,000 in 2020 figures) to print 50,000 copies and distribute them around the country to encourage settlers to come to the new state.

U. S. State Quarters Explained

## 48 WEST VIRGINIA

West Virginia's quarter features the beauty of the New River Gorge, and the New River Gorge Bridge. In December 2020 it became a national park.

The bridge was completed in 1977 and is both beautiful and practical. As a piece of structural art in a dramatic setting, it is one of the most photographed places in the state. On a practical level reduced a 40-minute drive down narrow mountain roads to something that took a leisurely minute to cross. New River Gorge is the longest single span bridge in the western hemisphere (3030 feet- over half a mile), and the third highest bridge in the United States.

During the annual Bridge Day festival people can walk across (about 80,000 people) and even rappel from the bridge (about 300 people.)

## 49 WISCONSIN

Wisconsin's state quarter focuses on the state's strong agricultural and dairy farming identity. The coin has the state motto "Forward", and features a cow, a wheel of cheese and an ear of corn.

Wisconsin did not start out a dairy state. Early settlers considered wheat the main crop, but insect infestation, soil exhaustion and cheaper wheat after the civil war from other states threatened their livelihood. This led them to try feed corn and dairy. By the end of the 1800s, more than 90% of the Wisconsin farmers raised cows.

Wisconsin dairy farms initially focused on cheese as an export, because it kept better than butter and milk. By 1915, Wisconsin led the country in butter and cheese production, as commercial refrigeration was introduced.

## 50 WYOMING

Wyoming's quarter features a bucking horse and rider, symbols of the state's Wild West heritage. Buffalo Bill Cody popularized Wyoming's era of cow boys and Indians with his Wild West shows. Buffalo Bill had been a scout, soldier, buffalo hunter, pony express rider and most famously a showman and entrepreneur. He also founded Cody, Wyoming.

The nickname "The Equality State" connects to both Buffalo Bill, and women's rights. In 1868, Buffalo Bill said, "If a woman can do the same work that a man can do and do it just as well, she should have the same pay." A year later the territory of Wyoming granted women the right to vote, a full 51 years before the 19th woman's suffrage amendment was passed.

## ABOUT THE AUTHOR

Jessica Miller loves to share trivia and works part time.
at a local grocery store in Cambria CA
on California's Central Coast.

Jessica is also a 25-year Reiki Master teacher, a prominent form of biofield
energy healing that started in Japan. She wrote.
Reiki's Birth place: A Site Guide to Kurama mountain,
and several Reiki Explorer class manuals.

Printed in Great Britain
by Amazon